15563

D0788022

discard

Chopin

Exploring Science

The Exploring Science series is designed to meet all the Attainment Targets in the National Science Curriculum for levels 3 to 6. **Exploring Weather**, in conjunction with **Exploring Soil and Rocks**, covers Attainment Target 9: The Earth and Atmosphere. The topics in each book are divided into knowledge and understanding sections, followed by exploration. Carefully planned Test Yourself questions at the end of each topic ensure that the student has mastered the appropriate level of attainment specified in the Curriculum.

30152000042245

EXPLORING WEATHER

Ed Catherall

Exploring Science

Electricity
Energy Sources
Light
Magnets
Soil and Rocks
Sound
Uses of Energy
Weather

Cover illustrations:
Top *A hang glider against the evening sky.*
Below left *A newspaper weather forecast map.*
Below right *Ice crystals formed on glass.*

Frontispiece *Holidaymakers enjoying the hot weather on Oahu, one of the Hawaiian Islands, USA.*

Editor: Elizabeth Spiers/Cally Chambers
Series designer: Ross George

First published in 1990 by
Wayland (Publishers) Ltd
61 Western Road, Hove
East Sussex BN3 1JD, England

©Copyright 1990 Wayland (Publishers) Ltd

British Library Cataloguing in Publication Data
Catherall, Ed. 1931–
    Exploring weather.
    1. Weather
    I. Title. II. Series
    551.5

ISBN 1 85210 791 X

Typeset by Direct Image Photosetting Ltd, Hove,
Sussex, England
Printed in Italy by G. Canale & C.S.p.A,, Turin
Bound in France by A.G.M.

Contents

THE WEATHER AND PEOPLE

Weather affects the lives of people all over the world. It affects the clothes we wear, the types of houses in which we live and the food we eat. The crops that we grow depend on the weather: too much rain causes floods; too little rain results in droughts. It can also be too cold or too hot for seedling plants to thrive.

Weather, therefore, has always been vital to life. Over the years, people have tried to predict the weather and developed sayings, or weather lore, to help them: for example, 'red sky at night is the shepherd's delight; red sky at morning is the shepherd's warning'. Most European and North American weather comes from the west. Red sky at night means that the Sun setting in the west is shining onto clouds in the east. These clouds have passed and as the sky is clear, good weather is coming. Red sky at morning means that the Sun rising in the east is lighting up clouds in the west. These clouds are approaching, bringing bad weather.

Another old saying with some truth in it is 'rain before seven; dry before eleven'. Usually, a weather front (see page 34) takes about four hours to pass over.

Plants and animals are used for weather advice: for example, 'many berries on the holly means a cold winter'. However, this is more likely to mean that there has been a good summer for the berries to form. Also, 'swallows fly low when cold weather is coming': swallows feed on insects on the wing. Insects cannot fly high in cold, windy weather. However, swallows fly low only if the cold weather has actually arrived. In general, animals and plants cannot be used to predict the weather.

According to weather lore, a red sky at night can mean that good weather is on the way.

ACTIVITY

HOW THE WEATHER AFFECTS US

YOU NEED

- **a scrapbook**
- **a large sheet of paper**
- **a collection of weather sayings**

1 Describe today's weather. Is the temperature in your room the same as the temperature outside? If not, why not? How is your room temperature controlled?

2 Are the clothes that you are wearing suitable to wear inside and outside?

What do you think the weather will be like in four hours' time? Will your clothes be suitable then?

3 Read your collection of weather sayings. Which, if any, do you think are true?

4 Are there any sayings that are local to your area? Ask older people; maybe they can remember some.

5 How could you test each of your weather sayings?

6 Start a scrapbook on weather. Include newspaper cuttings of the weather worldwide.

7 Use a large sheet of paper to start a weather chart.

8 Record the weather daily for a month. This book will help you to increase the accuracy of your observations.

Winters in Canada are extremely cold. These children in Ontario have to dress up warmly to go to school.

TEST YOURSELF

1. Describe a natural disaster that was caused by the weather.
2. What do you think would be ideal weather to grow crops in your district?
3. Find out about and describe the types of house that people live in to cope with their climates.

AIR IS ALL AROUND US

The Earth is surrounded by an envelope of air called the atmosphere. This consists of different layers. The layer nearest the ground is called the troposphere. It is only 10 km thick, which is not much higher than the top of Mount Everest. Near the equator, the troposphere is thicker; often more than 16 km. This layer contains enough of the gas, called oxygen, that we need to breathe.

Above the troposphere is the stratosphere, which reaches a height of 50 km above the Earth's surface. In this layer, the air does not contain enough oxygen for us to breathe properly. The temperature of −60°C is far too cold to hold any moisture, so there are no clouds here.

The atmosphere does more than provide us with our weather. It is essential to life on our planet. Apart from providing us with vital gases to breathe, it acts as a blanket, keeping out half the heat from the Sun. A lot of the Sun's harmful ultraviolet rays are absorbed by ozone, a type of oxygen. The stratosphere contains quite a large amount of ozone in a layer between 20 and 35 km above the ground.

The air blanket, with its clouds in the lowest layer, also keeps the warmth in at night and the heat out during the day. This stops the day and night temperatures from changing too much. This would threaten life. The clouds also contain water, which is essential to life.

Below *The atmosphere is made up of five layers − the troposphere, stratosphere, mesosphere, thermosphere and exosphere. The exosphere, above a height of about 500 km, is where the atmosphere merges into interplanetary space.*

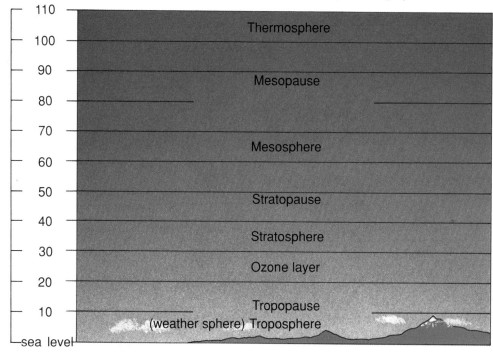

Thermosphere

Mesopause

Mesosphere

Stratopause

Stratosphere

Ozone layer

Tropopause
(weather sphere) Troposphere

110
100
90
80
70
60
50
40
30
20
10
sea level

Height in kilometres

Less oxygen in atmosphere

ACTIVITY

YOU NEED

- **clear plastic or glass bottles**
- **water**
- **a large plastic bowl**

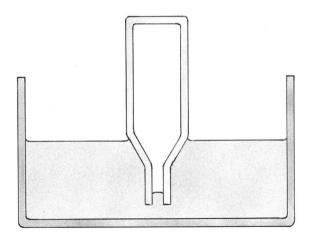

1 Half fill the bowl with water.
2 Take an empty plastic or glass bottle.
3 Turn the bottle upside down. Plunge the neck straight down into the bowl of water. Does water go into the empty bottle?

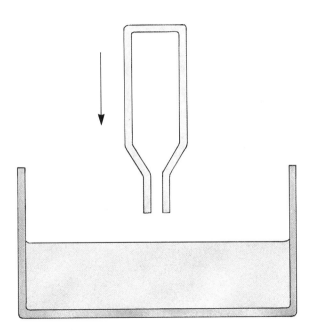

5 What happens if you let go of the bottle? Why?
6 Plunge the 'empty' bottle, upside down, into the water again.
7 Turn the bottle, so that the neck turns slightly upwards. What happens?

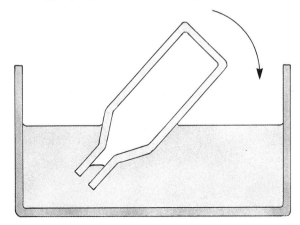

4 Push the bottle deeper into the water. What do you feel?

8 What comes out of your 'empty' bottle? What is inside it?

TEST YOURSELF

1. What is the lowest layer of the atmosphere called? How thick is it?
2. Why is the weather only in the lowest layer of the atmosphere?
3. Why is the atmosphere essential for life on Earth?

SUNSHINE AND TEMPERATURE

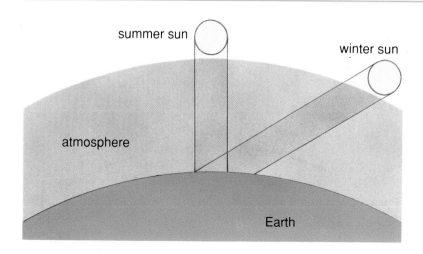

summer sun

winter sun

atmosphere

Earth

Temperatures are higher in summer than in winter. In summer the Sun is more directly overhead and the rays are concentrated on the Earth's surface. In winter the Sun is lower in the sky. Its rays have to travel a greater distance through the atmosphere, and they are less concentrated on the Earth's surface, so the weather is cooler.

Almost all the heat on Earth comes from the Sun. When it is directly above a point on the Earth's surface, the Sun's rays have the shortest journey through the atmosphere, so less heat is lost. This is when it is midday. As the Earth spins round, the distance that the Sun's rays have to travel through the atmosphere to reach the same point increases, and the temperature becomes cooler.

The Earth circles around the Sun once a year. The axis around which the Earth spins (once every 24 hours) is tilted. Because of this the seasons vary in different parts of the world. When the Sun is overhead at noon

on the Tropic of Cancer, it is the Summer Solstice in the northern hemisphere and the Winter Solstice in the southern hemisphere. Six months later, when the Sun is overhead at noon on the Tropic of Capricorn, it is the Winter Solstice in the northern hemisphere and the Summer Solstice in the south.

The Earth is curved, so the Sun's rays always have further to travel through the atmosphere over the poles than anywhere else in the world. The Sun's rays always have the shortest distance to travel over the equator. The temperature decreases from the equator to the poles. The equator is always hot, and the poles are always cold.

WHAT IS THE TEMPERATURE TODAY?

YOU NEED

- **a thermometer**
- **a sunny day**

---

1 Measure the temperature on the ground in the sun and in the shade.

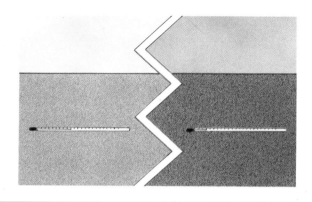

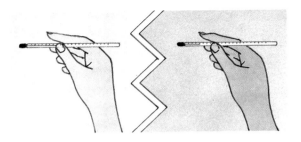

2 Measure the temperature of the air in the sun and in the shade.
3 How does the air temperature compare with the ground temperature?
4 Record these temperatures every hour throughout the day. Which was the hottest hour? Why do you think this is?

TEMPERATURES AROUND THE WORLD

YOU NEED

- **a strong flashlight**
- **a globe of the world**
- **a sheet of white paper**

1 Hold the sheet of paper vertically in front of the flashlight. What shape is the spot of light on the paper?

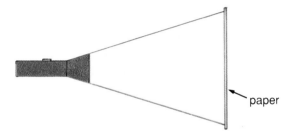

paper

2 Tilt the paper slightly. What happens to the light?
3 Compare how far the light from the edges of the light beam has to travel to the paper. If this were the Sun, which part of the paper would be hottest? Which part would be coldest?

4 Find where you live on the globe of the world.
5 Hold your flashlight over the Tropic of Cancer and shine it onto the place where you live. Notice what happens to the spot of light.

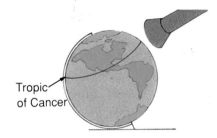

Tropic of Cancer

6 Now shine the flashlight from the equator. How is this different?

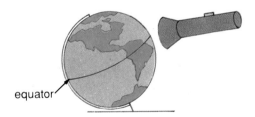

equator

7 Shine the flashlight from the Tropic of Capricorn. What happens to the spot of light? Where is the Sun when it is the Summer Solstice?

TEST YOURSELF

1. Where does the Earth's heat come from?
2. Where is the Sun at the time of the Winter Solstice?
3. Explain why it is hotter at the equator than at the poles.

AIR CURRENTS

When the Sun shines on the Earth, part of the Sun's energy, in the form of heat, is absorbed by the Earth. The land heats up faster than the sea, because the sea moves constantly. Air that is in contact with the land heats up faster than air over the sea.

When air is heated, it expands, taking up more space. The air particles move further apart, so the air becomes thinner and lighter; we say it is at low pressure. Because of this, the heated air rises above the surrounding air. This is called a thermal air current. You can often see gliders or birds circling around in rising air currents.

The Earth spins from east to west, and this spin affects the movement of the air. In the northern hemisphere, a region of rising warm air spins in an anticlockwise direction. This area of spinning low pressure air is also called a depression.

The warm air rises and gets cooler as it leaves the Earth's surface. Eventually, it becomes cold air. The particles in the air move closer together as the air cools. The air contracts, takes up less space and becomes denser and heavier. This air is at high pressure. As it sinks down towards the Earth, the high-pressure air flows into the depression. This is spinning anticlockwise,

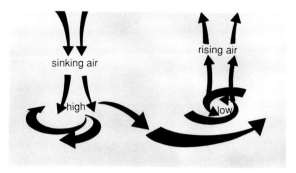

so the high-pressure. cold anticyclone spins clockwise as its air rushes into the depression. A depression spins clockwise and an anticyclone spins anti-clockwise.

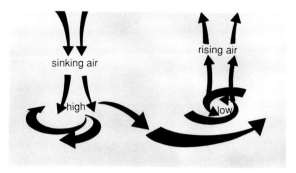

Hang gliders make use of rising air thermals to lift them higher into the sky.

ACTIVITIES

HOT AIR RISES

YOU NEED

- **a circular plate**
- **metal foil**
- **an electric toaster**
- **a pair of scissors**
- **thread**

WARNING: be careful when using the electric toaster. Ask an adult to help you.

1 Place the plate on the metal foil and draw around it. Cut out the foil circle.

2 Draw a spiral in the circle, about 2 cm wide. Use scissors to cut out the spiral.

3 Make a small hole in the middle of the spiral. Tie thread to the hole so that the spiral can be hung up.

4 Hold the spiral over an electric toaster that is turned off.

5 Turn on the toaster. What happens to the spiral? As the toaster heats up, take care that the hot air does not burn your hand.

LAND HEATS UP FASTER THAN THE SEA

YOU NEED

- **2 large identical plastic tubs**
- **water**
- **dry soil with the stones removed**
- **2 thermometers**
- **a sunny day**

1 Fill one tub with dry soil. Fill the other tub with water.

2 Carefully put a thermometer into each tub. Record the temperatures of the soil and the water.

3 Place both tubs in the sun.

4 Record the temperatures again after 30 minutes. Which heated faster?

5 Record the temperature in another 30 minutes.

	Start	after 30 mins.	after 1 hour
Temperature of soil (°C)			
Temperature of water (°C)			

6 Put both tubs in the shade. Which cools faster: the soil or the water?

TEST YOURSELF

1. Why does a thermal air current rise?

2. In which direction does a depression spin in the northern hemisphere?

3. Why does cool air have a higher pressure than warm air?

WORLD WEATHER PATTERNS

Air rises over the hot equator and sinks over the cold polar regions. This gives a band of low pressure at the equator and high pressure over the poles. There are three main systems of winds between the poles and the equator. The Polar Easterlies blow from the poles towards the temperate regions; the Westerlies blow away from the tropics towards the temperate zones; and the Trade Winds blow from the tropics towards the equator.

SEA BREEZES

On an island in summer, the Sun heats the land and it becomes hotter than the sea. Hot air rises over the land. Cool air is drawn in from the sea to replace the rising hot air. This creates an onshore (moving inland) sea breeze. The rising hot air is pulled high over the sea to replace the air drawn onto the land as a sea breeze. This cold air sinks and the wind cycle is complete. If the land cools rapidly at night, the sea is now warmer than the land. Warm air rises from the sea. Cool air is drawn from the land to replace this rising hot air. This creates an offshore wind.

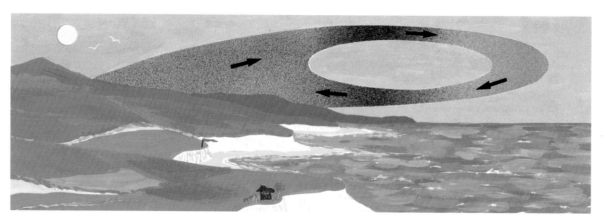

Above During the day warm air rises over the land and draws in a cool onshore breeze.
Below At night warm air rises over the sea causing a cool offshore breeze.

ACTIVITY

YOU NEED

- **a globe of the Earth**
- **a world atlas**
- **a recent newspaper**

1 Find the equator on the globe. Which major cities are near the equator?
2 Find the 30° and 60° latitudes. The temperate zone is between these two lines. Which major cities are near these latitudes?

3 Look in the newspaper for major city temperatures. What were the temperatures for these cities? Where are they? How do they compare with the area in which you live?
4 Look in the atlas for wind patterns. Some famous winds are the Doldrums at the equator, the Westerlies and the Trade Winds. Notice that the Westerlies are called the Roaring Forties in the southern hemisphere.
5 Look in your atlas for the major ocean currents. Compare them with the wind patterns. What do you notice?

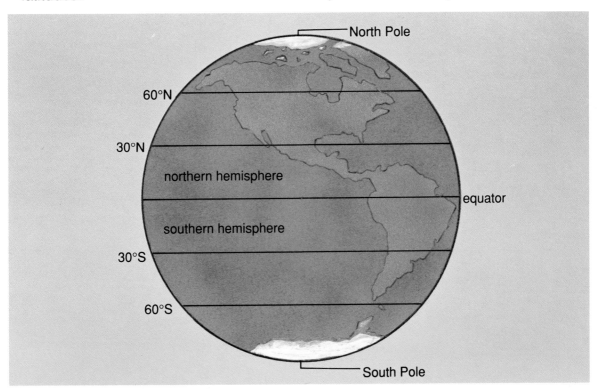

TEST YOURSELF

1. Which winds blow from the tropics towards the equator?
2. Draw a globe of the Earth and mark in the world's main wind systems.
3. Describe how sea breezes blow on an island.

THE WIND

Wherever you live, the wind comes from one main direction and is called the prevailing wind. It is caused by the world wind patterns (see page 14). However, this general direction can change, depending on the air currents at the time and whether the wind in these currents is moving in a clockwise or anticlockwise direction. Variations are also caused by large areas of water, such as oceans and lakes (see page 14). Hills and mountains divert the wind upwards, over them, and then down the other side. Valleys channel the wind; buildings and tall trees act as windbreaks, or cause the wind to swirl around, rather as the tide swirls around a rock on the beach.

In 1805, Sir Francis Beaufort, an Englishman, devised the Beaufort scale to estimate wind speeds. Here, you measure the general wind speed over ten minutes, ignoring the gusts.

Above *Mountain ranges, such as the Southern Alps in New Zealand, affect wind direction. They divert winds up and over them.*

Beaufort scale		Wind speed (kph)	Signs to look for
0	Calm	0-2	Smoke rises up
1	Light air	2-5	Smoke drifts
2	Light breeze	6-13	Leaves move; wind just felt on face
3	Gentle breeze	14-20	Leaves move constantly
4	Moderate breeze	21-30	Small branches move; flags flap
5	Fresh breeze	31-40	Small leafy trees sway
6	Strong breeze	41-50	Large branches move
7	Near gale	51-60	Whole trees sway
8	Fresh gale	61-75	Twigs break off trees
9	Strong gale	76-85	Large branches break off; house damage
10	Storm	86-100	Trees uprooted; major house damage
11	Violent storm	100-120	Widespread damage
12	Hurricane	120+	Disaster

Wind-speed scale	
Angle	kph
90°	0
85°	9
80°	13
70°	19
60°	24
50°	29
40°	34
35°	38
30°	42
25°	46
20°	52

ACTIVITY

WIND SPEED

YOU NEED

- **a table-tennis ball**
- **thread**
- **sticky tape**
- **a small spirit level**
- **a protractor**
- **a plastic bag**
- **a windy day**

1 Tape a length of thread to the table-tennis ball.
2 Tape the other end of the thread to the mid-point of the protractor. Check that the ball swings freely.
3 Tape the spirit level to the side of the protractor. You have made an anemometer (wind-speed meter).

4 Cut off the bottom of your plastic bag.
5 Hold up your plastic bag above your head. Hold it open. See which way it turns. This is the wind direction.

6 Hold your anemometer in the wind. Go into the open, away from trees and buildings, to do this.
7 Point the spirit level in the direction from which the wind is coming.

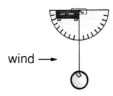

wind →

8 Check that the spirit-level bubble is in the centre.
9 Ask a friend to read off the angle that the ball and thread make, when the wind blows.

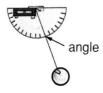

angle

10 Calculate the wind speed from the chart on page 16.
11 Measure the average wind speed by taking ten readings over ten minutes.
12 Use the Beaufort scale on the opposite page to measure wind speed. Compare your record with this reading. Look for the signs given for that wind speed.

TEST YOURSELF

1. What does prevailing wind mean?
2. What can alter the direction of the prevailing wind?
3. What is the Beaufort scale?

WATER IN THE AIR

As saturated air cools and moisture condenses, fogs and mists may form, especially where the air is still.

Dry air absorbs (takes up) water by evaporation. Any water that is open to dry air will evaporate. Large quantities of water are absorbed from the sea, lakes, ponds, rivers, puddles and streams. Plants, especially trees, give off water; so does damp earth.

Evaporated water is held in the air as invisible water vapour. The amount of water vapour that the air will hold depends on its temperature. Hot air holds more water than cold air. However, there is a maximum amount of water vapour that the air will hold at a particular temperature: for example, air at 28°C holds slightly less water than air at 30°C. We say that the air is saturated when it will not absorb any more water vapour. When the air is saturated, your clothes feel damp and your sweat sticks to your body, as it cannot evaporate.

The difference between the actual amount of water vapour in the air and the amount of water vapour in saturated air is called the relative humidity. When the air is saturated, the relative humidity is 100 per cent.

If there is half the amount of water vapour in the air, the humidity is halved, so the relative humidity is 50 per cent.

If the saturated air cools down, it loses some of its water vapour. This invisible water vapour condenses (turns into water). Tiny droplets of water appear in the air, and elsewhere, when this happens.

ACTIVITIES

AIR 'DRIES UP' WATER

YOU NEED

- **a saucer**
- **a bowl**
- **a cup**
- **water**
- **a measuring cylinder**
- **a sunny day**

1 Use the measuring cylinder to put the same quantity of water into each of the three containers.

2 Put the containers on the window sill, or outside.

3 Which container has the largest water surface?
4 Look at the water in each container after 1 hour.
5 Pour the water from the cup into the measuring cylinder. How much is left?

6 Repeat this for the saucer and the bowl.
7 Compare the amount of water lost to the size of the water surface. Is there a pattern in your results?

SATURATED AIR

YOU NEED

- **2 identical small saucers**
- **a measuring cylinder**
- **water**
- **a plastic tub that will cover one saucer**

1 Use the measuring cylinder to put the same quantity of water into both saucers.
2 Put them in the shade and cover one with the tub.

3 After 1 hour, measure the amount of water in both saucers.
4 Which saucer has had more water evaporated from it?
5 Look in the plastic tub. Is there any water sticking to the sides of the tub? The tub traps the air over the saucer and this trapped air soon becomes saturated.

TEST YOURSELF

1. Which holds more water vapour: warm or cool air?
2. What is relative humidity?
3. What happens when saturated air is cooled?

FROST, MIST AND FOG

Water can be found in three forms: solid ice, liquid water and the gas, water vapour. Warm air contains this gas (see page 18). Even if warm air is not saturated, it still contains a lot of water vapour. As the temperature falls, so the air becomes more humid, until it becomes saturated. If the air cools further, then some of the water vapour condenses out to make water droplets. The temperature at which the water vapour condenses is called the dew point.

If the dew point is below freezing point, 0°C, the water will condense out in the form of ice crystals, covering everything in frost. This usually happens on clear, cold nights, when the ground loses heat rapidly. The air in contact with the ground is cooled. In temperate lands, this happens in winter, early spring and late autumn.

Fog and mist form when warm, moist air comes in contact with cold ground. As the ground cools at night, fog forms where the air is saturated, such as over rivers, lakes and ponds. Freezing fog is formed when water droplets are at 0°C or even a degree lower. These 'supercooled' droplets will remain liquid until they touch a cold surface, where they turn to ice.

Smog is a mixture of fog and smoke, and the dust and pollution from cities.

Above Water vapour can condense into droplets on something as fine as a spider's web.

Left Frost on the edge of this maple leaf formed when the dew point was below freezing (0°C) and water condensed into ice crystals.

ACTIVITY

CONDENSATION

YOU NEED

- **a refrigerator**
- **a dry metal can**
- **a bottle**
- **ice cubes**
- **a clean glass**
- **a mirror**
- **a large glass jar**

1 Clean the mirror and the glass.
2 Put them in the refrigerator for ten minutes.
3 Take out the mirror. Breathe on it. What do you see?

4 Take out the glass. Stand it on a table. What happens when the glass warms up?

5 Put ice cubes in the dry can. Watch the outside of the can. What can you see?

6 Fill the clean bottle with warm water from the tap. Leave the bottle for several minutes. Pour out the water.
7 Stand a large ice cube on the top of the bottle. Can you see the cloud forming in the air just under the ice cube?

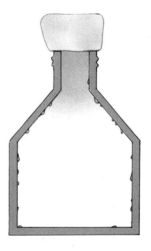

TEST YOURSELF

1. What is the dew point?
2. Describe how frost forms.
3. How does fog form? What turns it into smog?

CLOUDS

Clouds are formed when saturated air cools. The excess water condenses out as tiny droplets of water. These droplets collide with others and get larger and heavier, until they fall as rain. Saturated air is caused by warm, moist air being carried into the upper atmosphere where it is colder, or by saturated air being forced up over the top of a mountain. That is why mountains often have clouds on them.

There are three basic types of cloud. The highest are made of tiny ice crystals and are called cirrus. These wispy clouds are often followed by lower layers of stratus. These are light-grey sheets of cloud. They are composed of fine water droplets that become larger and larger as they collide with each other. There are three layers of stratus cloud; altostratus, nimbostratus and the lowest layer, stratus.

The third kind of cloud is cumulus. These look like white, fluffy cauliflowers with a flat base. They are caused by an uprush of air. If this is violent, the cloud will develop into the storm cloud cumulonimbus, which is dark and gives lightning, thunder and rain.

Below *Low, stormy nimbostratus clouds bring heavy rain or snow.*

There are all sorts of cloud combinations. Basically, white clouds are made of ice crystals. Light-grey clouds have small water droplets that get bigger and bigger so that the cloud gets darker and blacker, until the droplets fall as rain.

Above *Cirrus are very high, wispy clouds made up of feathery ice crystals.*

Below *This is often called a 'mackerel sky' because the ripples of cloud look like fish scales. These cirrocumulus clouds bring unsettled weather.*

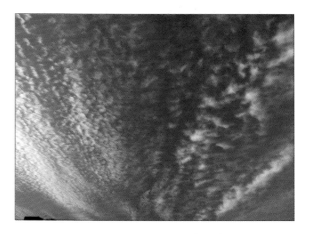

Above *Clusters of small white cumulus clouds are usually a sign of fair weather.*

ACTIVITY

A CLOUD DISPLAY

YOU NEED

• **pictures of clouds**

1 Identify your cloud pictures.

2 Find out all you can about each cloud. Record this information in your own words.
3 Display your pictures with the information about them.
4 Record the clouds that you see every day, and the weather. Record the time that you saw each cloud. Record which way the wind was blowing and how the cloud types changed.

TEST YOURSELF

1. Why are clouds often seen on the tops of mountains?
2. What are the three basic types of cloud?
3. Which cloud gives thunder and lightning?

RAIN

Rain forms in two ways. In the tropics, warm clouds rise, cool and their water droplets condense. These liquid droplets collide with others, getting larger and larger, until the large drops break up into smaller ones. Each of these then grows larger by colliding with others. Eventually, when they move to cooler air, these drops fall as rain.

In cooler, temperate regions, the temperature of the cloud may drop to freezing point or lower. This makes the tiny water droplets freeze. Any surrounding water vapour condenses onto the frozen droplets. These get larger and heavier and eventually drop down to earth. As they fall, they get warmer, melt and reach the ground as raindrops.

There are three types of rainfall: convection, relief and frontal (cyclonic).

Convection rain is caused by heat. Hot air rises and cools, causing the water vapour to condense and fall as rain. This causes showers in temperate regions, or very heavy rain in the tropics.

Relief rain (orographic rain) occurs when moist air is blown up over mountains and hills. Here, it rises and cools to form rain on the side of the mountain from which the wind comes. The far side of the mountain is dry, because the rain has already fallen on the other side. This is the 'rain shadow'.

The third kind of rain, frontal rain, is due to the changes in temperature caused by the advance of weather fronts (see page 34).

As saturated air rises over mountains and the temperature drops with altitude, the water vapour condenses and falls as relief rain.

ACTIVITY

MAKING A RAIN GAUGE

YOU NEED

- **a straight-sided glass jar**
- **sticky tape**
- **a plastic funnel that fits in the glass jar**
- **a ruler**
- **modelling clay**

1 Use your ruler to draw a metric scale in millimetres on paper.
2 Stick this scale on the outside of the jar. Make sure the scale starts above the thickness of the bottom of the jar. Stick the scale facing inwards so that you can read it by looking through the jar.

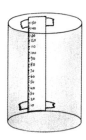

3 Place the funnel in the top of the jar.
4 Make sure it is fixed and water-tight by putting a layer of modelling clay between the jar and the funnel.

5 Pour water down the funnel and practise reading different water levels.

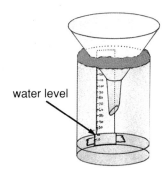

water level

6 Take off the funnel and clay, empty the jar and dry it with a cloth.
7 Put the funnel and clay back in place.
8 Place your rain gauge outside to collect rainwater.
9 Record the depth of rain in your rain gauge each day.
10 Remember to empty your rain gauge each day.
11 Record your results as a bar graph.

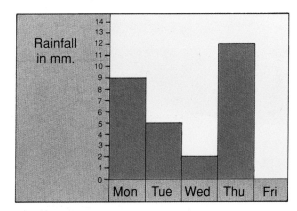

Rainfall in mm.

TEST YOURSELF

1. How is rain formed in temperate regions?
2. What is convection rain?
3. What is relief, or orographic, rain? Give an example of where you might expect this rain to fall.

SNOW AND HAIL

Snow forms when tiny droplets of water condense and freeze into ice crystals. Then, more ice crystals freeze onto the original crystals. Many crystals have to be joined together to form a snowflake. If the air is very cold, the snowflake will be small, giving dry, powdery snow. This can be cleared by a snow-blower.

If the air temperature is below 4°C, snow can fall, but it will only make wet, melting snow at the higher temperatures. At really freezing temperatures, the air is very dry. Snow may reach the ground from air at a temperature as high as 7°C, but it melts at once.

The air currents inside a large, towering cumulonimbus thundercloud are very violent and rise and fall. A falling raindrop can be carried up to the top of the cloud, where it freezes to form a hailstone. This small hailstone can start to fall and be carried up again, having another layer of ice added to it. In this way, hailstones can become larger and larger, sometimes reaching the size of golf balls, when they can break glass and damage cars. Luckily, most hailstones rarely get bigger than the size of peas.

Above Snow crystals seen through a microscope. Snow crystals are always six-sided and every one is a different shape.

Left Wet melting snow is just right for making snowballs.

ACTIVITY

THE SHAPE OF A SNOW CRYSTAL

YOU NEED

- **a saucer**
- **scissors**
- **white paper**

1 Put the saucer onto the sheet of white paper. Draw around the saucer.

2 Remove the saucer and cut out the circle of white paper.

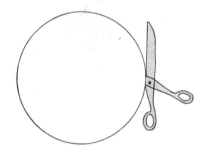

3 Fold the circle in half.

4 Fold the half-circle into thirds by bending one segment over to match an equal-sized segment. Fold it inwards.

5 Fold the other segment inwards.

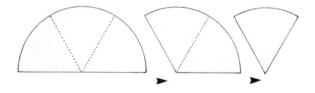

6 Open out your circle and check that the segments are equal. Cut halfway along each fold from the outside inwards.

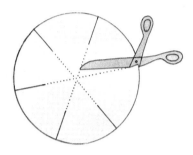

7 Fold the paper up again, then fold it over once more.

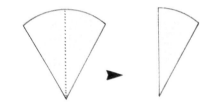

8 Cut the corners off the folded paper.

9 Cut pieces out of both straight sides.

10 Open out your paper. You have made a snow crystal shape. Make other snow crystals with different designs.

TEST YOURSELF

1. Draw the pattern of a snow crystal.

2. Describe how snowflakes are formed.

3. How are hailstones made?

THE WATER CYCLE

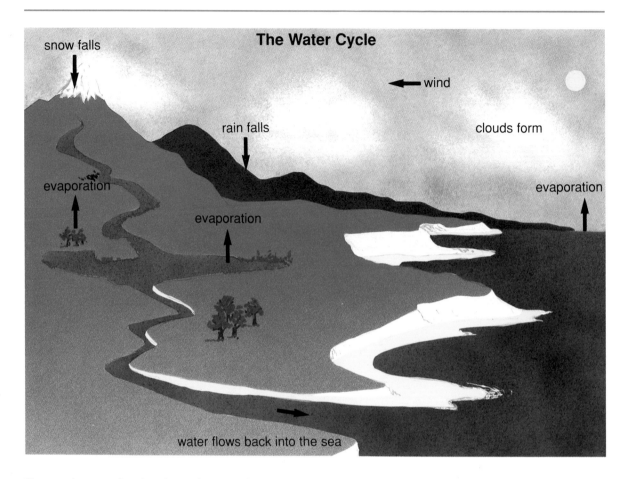

The Water Cycle

snow falls

wind

rain falls

clouds form

evaporation

evaporation

evaporation

water flows back into the sea

Every plant and animal needs water in order to survive. The water cycle provides the Earth with a continual supply of fresh water.

About two-thirds of the Earth's surface is covered by oceans. The Sun's rays heat the oceans and cause some of the water to evaporate into water vapour, much of which condenses and forms clouds (see page 22). Clouds that form over the oceans often shed rain that falls straight back into the oceans, but some rainclouds are blown towards land.

The Sun's rays also heat up the land and evaporate water from lakes, rivers and streams. When animals and humans breathe, they put water vapour into the air. You can see the effect of this when you breathe out on a cold, clear day. Your breath forms a cloud because the warm, moist air you breathe out is cooled below its dew point (see page 20). Plants, especially trees, draw in water from the soil through their roots. Later this water evaporates from their leaves.

The water cycle is completed when water that has evaporated from land and sea condenses and falls back to Earth as precipitation (rain, snow and hail). This precipitation returns the water to the seas, lakes, rivers, soil and, eventually, to the plants and animals. This process happens all the time. Because of air currents and world weather patterns, water evaporated from one place will usually fall somewhere far away.

ACTIVITY

MEASURING THE HUMIDITY OF THE AIR

YOU NEED

- **2 thermometers**
- **cotton wool**
- **water**
- **2 rubber bands**
- **a plastic tub**
- **a dry, sunny day**

---

1 Wrap the bulb of both thermometers in the same amount of cotton wool.
2 Use rubber bands to hold the cotton wool to the thermometers.
3 Let the end of the cotton wool hang down.
4 Soak the cotton wool on one thermometer with water. Leave the other thermometer dry.
5 Put water in the plastic tub. Place it under the wet thermometer to keep the cotton wool wet.

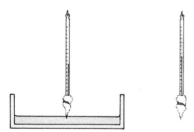

6 Hang both thermometers outside in the shade. Leave them for 30 minutes.

7 Read the temperatures of both thermometers. Notice that the wet thermometer registers a cooler temperature than the dry thermometer.
8 Record both temperatures.
9 Work out the difference in temperature between the two thermometers.

Wet thermometer (°C)	
Dry thermometer (°C)	
Difference between wet and dry thermometers (°C)	

10 Use the chart below to calculate the humidity of the air.

Humidity chart

		Dry temperature		
		10-14°C	15-19°C	20-25°C
Difference between wet and dry thermometers	1°C	85%	90%	90%
	2°C	75%	80%	80%
	3°C	60%	65%	70%
	4°C	50%	60%	65%
	5°C	40%	50%	55%
	6°C	30%	40%	45%
	7°C	15%	30%	40%
	8°C	5%	20%	30%
	9°C	0%	10%	25%
	10°C	0%	5%	20%

11 Repeat your recordings at different times of the day.

TEST YOURSELF

1. Describe the water cycle. Draw a picture to help you.
2. What is the energy that drives the water cycle?
3. Why is the water cycle so important?

LIGHTS IN THE SKY

There are many different light effects in the sky. They usually depend on the weather. Here are some that you will probably have seen.

Rainbows are caused by sunlight striking falling raindrops. A sunray strikes the top or bottom of a raindrop and the light is bent inwards, towards the middle of the drop. It is then reflected off the back of the raindrop and the light is bent again as the ray leaves the drop. White light, such as sunlight, is made up of the colours of the spectrum. There are seven main colours: red, orange, yellow, green, blue, indigo and violet. The light-bending separates them, forming the band of colours we call a rainbow.

Sun haloes are similar, but here, the Sun's rays are passing through ice crystals, like those found in cirrus clouds. The tiny crystals act like cut diamonds, bending the light and then reflecting it.

Lightning is caused by violent air currents inside a cumulonimbus cloud. These air currents rub the water drops, hailstones or ice crystals together and the cloud becomes charged with static electricity. Positive charges collect at the top of the cloud and negative charges at the bottom. The charges eventually build up so much that the negative charge jumps. It does this either inside the cloud, giving sheet lightning, or down to the ground, giving forked lightning.

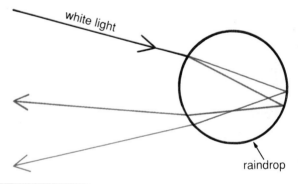

white light

raindrop

Above *When white light from the Sun strikes a raindrop, the light is split into the colours of the spectrum (red, orange, yellow, green blue, indigo and violet). In the diagram, only red and violet light are shown; the other colours lie between the two, in order.*

Left *The Moon can sometimes appear to have a halo. This is created by light passing through ice crystals in very high clouds.*

ACTIVITY

MAKING A RAINBOW

YOU NEED

- **a clean glass tumbler**
- **water**
- **paints**
- **a large sheet of paper**
- **sunshine**

---

1 Stand a glass full of water on a window sill in bright sunlight.

2 Place the sheet of paper on the floor below the window sill.
3 Move the glass until you see the rainbow on the paper.

4 Identify the colours of the rainbow. Paint these colours in a picture.

5 Next time you see a weather rainbow, look to see where the Sun and rainclouds are. Sometimes you can see a double rainbow. This is a normal rainbow, with another, paler rainbow outside it, with the colours in reverse order.

Rainbows can often be seen if the Sun shines while it is still raining. To see a rainbow clearly, stand with your back to the Sun and look towards the falling raindrops.

TEST YOURSELF

1. How are rainbows made?
2. What are sun haloes and how are they caused?
3. How is lightning caused?

AIR PRESSURE AND AIR MASSES

Over 300 years ago the Italian scientist Evangelista Torricelli discovered that the air presses on everything. He invented the barometer to measure air pressure. At sea level, the pressure is about 1 kg per square centimetre. This is the same as having a 1 kg weight standing on a patch of ground that is 1 square centimetre large. The air pressure falls as you get higher above the Earth's surface. At about 5,000 m, the air pressure is about half its value at sea level. This is because there are fewer air particles to cause pressure.

Dry air has high pressure, but air saturated with water vapour has a lower pressure. This is because the water vapour takes up space, forcing the air particles apart, so that there is less air there to create the pressure.

Air pressure enables us to study air masses. These huge areas of air are named after the kind of climate they come from. If the air mass is over the sea it is called maritime. If the air mass is over land, it is called continental.

There are four main types of air mass in the world. Tropical continental is warm, dry, high pressure. Tropical maritime is warm, moist, low pressure. Polar continental is cold, dry, high pressure. Polar maritime is cold and fairly moist low pressure. These air masses are moved by the world wind patterns. Where two air masses meet, it is called a front.

Above A weather balloon (see page 40) like this one at a weather station in Colorado, USA, can be sent up 30 km into the stratosphere to record changes in air pressure.

Right Many people have a barometer in their home. Most barometers give a reading in millibars (mb).

ACTIVITY

AIR PRESSURE

YOU NEED

- **a barometer**
- **weather maps**

---

1 Read the air pressure with your barometer.

2 Take the air pressure reading every 3 hours, until the air pressure changes. Is the air pressure rising or falling? What is happening to the weather?

Time	Air pressure	Weather summary
9.00		
12.00		
15.00		

3 Look at some weather maps. Places with the same air pressure are joined by a line called an isobar.

4 Find where you live on a weather map. What is the air pressure in the area where you live?

5 Which other places have the same pressure? Which places are showing a higher or lower pressure?

6 Find a low-pressure area. What is the lowest pressure? Notice that the pressure goes down in the middle of this area.

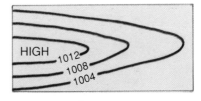

7 Find a high-pressure area. Where is the highest pressure area? Notice that the pressure goes up in the middle. The closer the isobars, the greater the wind speed.

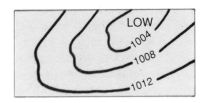

In the northern hemisphere, winds blow clockwise around a high-pressure region and anticlockwise around a low-pressure region.

In the southern hemisphere, winds blow clockwise around a low-pressure area and anticlockwise around a high-pressure area.

TEST YOURSELF

1. Which instrument do you use to measure air pressure?
2. Which gives the higher pressure: wet or dry air?
3. Describe the four main air masses of the world.

A WARM FRONT

A front is the dividing line between the warm, moist air of a depression (area of low pressure) and the cold, dry air of an anticyclone (area of high pressure). The leading edge of a depression is called the warm front.

When two large air masses meet, moving in opposite directions, the warm, moist air mass rises above the denser, dry air mass. As it rises the water vapour condenses, forming a series of different cloud types. The clouds become lower and thicker, bringing rain.

Below *This diagram shows four towns, each 300 km apart, in the path of a warm front.*

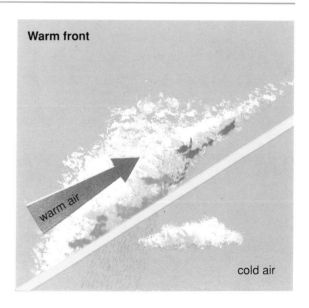

Warm front

warm air

cold air

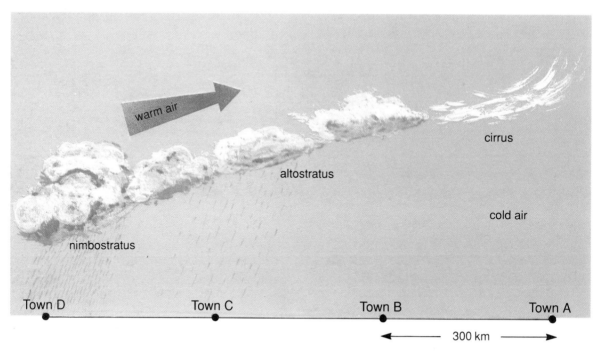

warm air

cirrus

altostratus

cold air

nimbostratus

Town D   Town C   Town B   Town A

300 km

Town A has clear, cold weather, with a few high cirrus clouds. Town B has thicker, lower clouds and the sky is grey. Town C has dark altostratus clouds with light drizzle.

Town D has nimbostratus clouds with heavy rain. When it stops raining it will be warm and humid. It will take about 12 hours for each town to get the weather from the town before.

ACTIVITY

SEARCHING FOR DEPRESSIONS

YOU NEED

- **weather maps from newspapers, for several days in a row**
- **a ruler**

Below *Weather forecasting is especially important for the safety of vessels at sea, and for people enjoying leisure activities like this international yachting event off New Zealand.*

1 Find a depression on the map. Where is its leading edge?
2 Look at the cities that the depression covers, from the front edge to the centre of the depression.
3 Predict the weather for each city (see page 34).
4 Look at the weather reports for these cities for several days. Does your prediction match those of the experts?
5 Look at the weather maps for several days. How does the weather change? Do the weather reports match the air-pressure charts?

TEST YOURSELF

1. Where do you find warm fronts?
2. How are warm fronts formed?
3. Predict the weather that is likely to occur as a warm front passes.

A COLD FRONT

Two fronts are formed around a depression: a warm front ahead and a cold front behind. The cold front marks the edge of approaching cold air. As the cold air moves forward it forces itself under the warm air like a huge wedge. As this happens, the water vapour in the warm front rises and condenses even faster. This sudden cooling creates the towering cumulonimbus thunderclouds. The weather will become stormy. Rain will continue as the front passes, then the barometer will rise. Gradually, bright, clear air will move forward as the clouds get thinner.

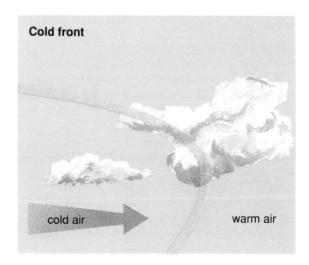

Cold front

cold air

warm air

Below These four towns, 200 km apart, are in the path of a cold front.

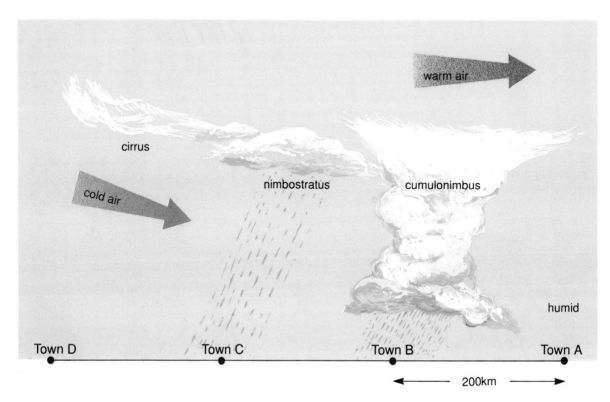

warm air

cirrus

cold air

nimbostratus

cumulonimbus

humid

Town D

Town C

Town B

Town A

200km

Town A has warm, moist air. Town B has large cumulonimbus clouds with thunderstorms and torrential rain. Town C has rain from nimbostratus clouds. Town D has bright, cool air.

ACTIVITY

YOU NEED

- **weather maps from newspapers for several days (which include anticyclones)**
- **a ruler**

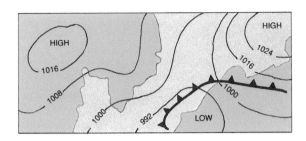

1 Where is the cold front on the map?
2 Which towns are under that leading edge?

3 What is the forecast for those towns?
4 Notice that high-pressure areas tend to be larger than low-pressure areas (see page 33).

The temperature outside does not always tell you how cold it feels. The speed of the wind makes a difference. It creates the wind-chill factor. If the wind blows hard, the temperature feels colder than the thermometer reading.

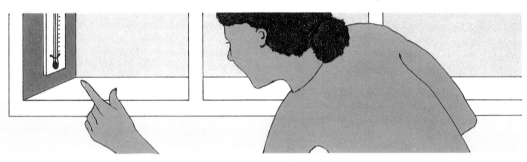

Wind chill chart	Outside temperature						
Wind speed (kph)	7°C	4°C	2°C	1°C	–4°C	–7°C	
8	6°C	3°C	0°C	–3°C	–6°C	–9°C	
16	1°C	–2°C	–6°C	–8°C	–12°C	–16°C	Wind
24	–2°C	–5°C	–9°C	–13°C	–19°C	–21°C	chill
32	–3°C	–7°C	–11°C	–16°C	–19°C	–23°C	temperature
40	–5°C	–9°C	–13°C	–17°C	–22°C	–26°C	
48	–6°C	–11°C	–14°C	–19°C	–23°C	–28°C	
56	–7°C	–11°C	–16°C	–20°C	–24°C	–29°C	

TEST YOURSELF

1. What is a cold front?
2. What weather would you expect to get as a cold front passes?
3. Draw a weather map with isobars, showing an anticyclone and a cold front.

JET STREAMS AND HURRICANES

Between 10 and 12 km above the Earth's surface, a wind blows, like a river of air. This is called the jet stream. There is a westerly jet stream in the northern and southern hemispheres, blowing towards the east. Both jet streams blow continuously, right around the world, between latitudes 40° and 70°. The northern jet stream is called the Polar Front Jet Stream. The wind in these jet streams blows at speeds from 100 kph to over 300 kph. Aircraft flying eastwards try to fly in the jet stream, in order to be carried along by it.

A hurricane is a severe storm. In China and Japan, it is called a typhoon. In India, it is called a cyclone and in Australia, a willy-willy. Hurricanes occur over tropical seas and develop as deep depressions. They spin anticlockwise in the northern hemisphere and clockwise in the southern hemisphere.

A hurricane with warmth and moisture in it will grow bigger and stronger, measuring up to 2,000 km across. The wind speed may reach 300 kph. The low-pressure centre is known as the eye of the storm. Here, the air is quite calm, compared with its surroundings.

If the storm strikes land, great damage is done on the coast. As the hurricane moves inland, it is without moisture from the sea and it slowly dies, the winds slacken and the eye fills in.

Tornadoes are small but very powerful whirlwinds that may form very suddenly within severe tropical storms. Wind speeds may reach up to 500 kph, far higher than in any hurricane.

Above Satellites (see page 40) are able to send back clear pictures of weather, like this one of Hurricane Pat over the Western Pacific.

Left A tornado may only last a few minutes but it is immensely powerful and can cause a lot of damage. The whirling funnel of wind extends down from the bottom of a cumulonimbus cloud like a length of hosepipe.

ACTIVITIES

JET STREAMS

YOU NEED

- **an airline timetable**
- **a globe or atlas of the world**

1 Use your timetable to find out the flight time of an aircraft going from London to New York.
2 Compare this with the time taken for the aircraft to travel from New York to London.
3 Remember to allow for the difference between London and New York local times. (An atlas will have a world map showing time zones).
4 Check the times of aircraft to and from London and Los Angeles; London and Vancouver. Remember to allow for time differences.
5 What do you notice about the times to and from these places?
6 Look at your globe or atlas. What is the general direction of each place from London?
7 What is the effect of the jet stream?
8 Try other flight times that you think will be affected by the jet stream.

HURRICANES

YOU NEED

- **newspaper reports about hurricanes**

1 Make a display of reports of hurricanes.
2 Record when and where they occurred. What was the maximum wind speed recorded? How much damage was done? Find out all you can about the storm.

Right In 1988, Hurricane Gilbert hit Jamaica. It was strong enough to overturn this aeroplane.

TEST YOURSELF

1. What is the jet stream?
2. What are hurricanes and what makes them grow?
3. What happens to hurricanes when they reach land?

FORECASTING THE WEATHER

In order to forecast what the weather will be like tomorrow, it is essential to know, in as much detail as possible, what the weather is like today.

People on the move need to know what kind of weather they will meet on their journeys. For this reason, there are weather reports for road traffic organizations, the police, ships at sea and airlines. Ships' captains and airline pilots spend a lot of time arranging their routes to take advantage of the weather. Farmers, power-supply engineers and road-maintenance workers all need accurate weather information.

In order to obtain all this information, weather satellites orbit the Earth, sending down information and pictures every 30 minutes. Free-flying balloons are sent to heights of up to 30 km above the Earth. They transmit temperature, air-pressure and humidity information back to the ground. The balloons are tracked to record how they move in the winds of the stratosphere. Weather stations on land and weather ships send in detailed weather maps and reports every six hours to meteorological centres.

Modern weather forecasting relies on computers to analyse the information from hundreds of weather stations and to highlight changes and trends. This enables the forecaster to predict future weather patterns, to give us tomorrow's weather forecast.

Left *TIROS weather satellites orbit the Earth and send back weather information at 2-hour intervals. TIROS stands for Television Infra-Red Orbital Satellite.*

ACTIVITY

YOU NEED

- **video recordings of television weather forecasts**
- **a video and monitor**
- **newspaper weather reports**

1 Look at the weather forecast on television.
2 What weather systems are illustrated?
3 What frontal systems are shown?
4 In which direction are these systems moving?
5 What forecast was given by the presenter?
6 What reasons were given for this forecast?
7 Which symbols were used?
8 Look at newspaper weather reports. What weather systems are shown?
9 Which weather symbols are used? What forecasts are given?
10 What is the weather like today? What type of weather would you expect tomorrow?
11 Draw a large weather map showing weather systems and symbols.

12 Display this map and give a weather forecast to your friends, pretending to be a weather presenter.

Above *A weather presenter shows us current weather patterns and gives us tomorrow's forecast.*

Below *Some examples of weather symbols. They may vary in different newspapers and on different television channels.*

cloudy - fine weather   rain   snow   temperature (°C)

TEST YOURSELF

1. Name three types of workers who find weather information essential.
2. What are weather balloons used for?
3. Describe how weather information is used to produce a weather forecast.

AIR POLLUTION

You will probably have read or heard a great deal about air pollution. Humans are constantly polluting the atmosphere. Politicians, scientists and ordinary people are becoming increasingly worried about the effects of this. We use large amounts of fossil fuels (gas, oil and coal) for a number of purposes. They are used for heating, to produce electricity, in industry and for our cars, trucks, trains and aircraft. When these fuels are burnt, gases are produced. These are mainly carbon dioxide, sulphur dioxide and oxides of nitrogen.

Acid rain is one seriously damaging result. The gases sulphur dioxide and oxides of nitrogen combine with water droplets in the air to give acid. When these droplets condense, they fall as acid rain. This can kill plants and life in rivers and lakes.

Certain chemicals released into the atmosphere can destroy the special oxygen compound in the ozone layer. This usually forms a protective blanket around the world, blocking out some of the harmful rays of the Sun. But where holes appear more of the harmful ultraviolet rays can reach the Earth's surface and could damage living things.

Below The purple patches in these satellite pictures show the growing hole in the ozone layer of our atmosphere over the South Pole.

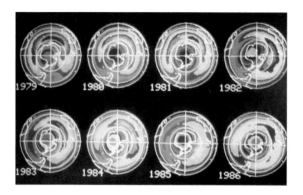

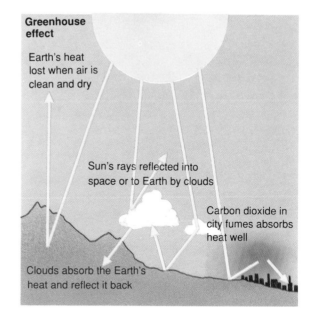

Greenhouse effect

Earth's heat lost when air is clean and dry

Sun's rays reflected into space or to Earth by clouds

Carbon dioxide in city fumes absorbs heat well

Clouds absorb the Earth's heat and reflect it back

You will have heard about the greenhouse effect. There are several pollutants that cause this, but the most important is carbon dioxide. Green plants take in carbon dioxide and give out oxygen. Animals do the opposite, and ideally there should be a balance. However, as vast areas of forest are cut down and cleared, and fossil fuels are burnt in large amounts, the level of carbon dioxide rises all over the world. This gas forms a layer in the atmosphere. The Sun's energy can penetrate this layer, but gets trapped, just as it would by the glass in a greenhouse. This causes the overall world temperature to rise. Living things that are sensitive to temperature changes could suffer seriously as a result. The extra heat could also melt the polar ice caps, causing flooding, as well as other harmful changes in world weather patterns.

People all over the world are trying to improve the situation, but, unfortunately, it is very expensive to stop the major pollutants from entering the atmosphere.

ACTIVITY

ACID RAIN

YOU NEED

- **2 red cabbage leaves**
- **a kettle**
- **a bowl**
- **a wooden spoon**
- **distilled water**
- **2 glass jars**
- **rainwater**
- **a measuring cylinder**

1 Tear the red cabbage leaves into small pieces. Put the cabbage pieces in a bowl.
2 Boil water in a kettle. Pour the hot water on the leaves until they are covered.

3 Carefully use the wooden spoon to squeeze the juice from the leaves into the hot water.

4 Let the cabbage stand for one hour.
5 Use the measuring cylinder to pour 20 ml of distilled water into one jar and 20 ml of rainwater into the other jar.

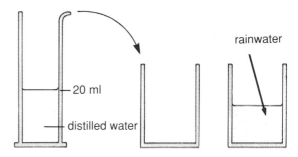

6 Add an equal amount of the purple cabbage juice to each jar. Watch for any change of colour.

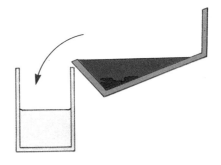

7 Compare the colour of the distilled water and the rainwater. If your rainwater turns red it is acid.

WARNING: take care when boiling water in a kettle. Ask an adult to help you.

TEST YOURSELF

1. What causes acid rain?
2. How is the gas carbon dioxide usually kept constant, or in balance, in our atmosphere?
3. What is the greenhouse effect?

CLIMATE AND AGRICULTURE

The world's population is constantly increasing. In AD 1600 there were only 500 million people in the world. By 1950, this had risen to 2,500 million. The numbers rise daily, and by the year 2000 the population will probably be over 6,000 million.

All these people have to be fed and housed. In order to do this, the world's forests are being cut down to provide land for agriculture, and wood for fuel and building. The forests are also cleared so that land can be mined, and roads, pipelines, power lines and dams can be built.

Cutting down the forests can seriously affect world weather. The leaves of forest trees release large amounts of moisture into the atmosphere — without them the local rainfall is reduced, which may result in droughts. The trees also take in large quantities of carbon dioxide, which helps to lessen the greenhouse effect (see page 42).

Forest trees have deep roots that hold the soil in place and prevent soil erosion. If trees are cut down on hillsides the exposed soil may be washed away by heavy rains, causing disastrous mudslides, the silting up of rivers, and possible flooding. When large areas of cleared forest land are ploughed up for crops, winds often blow away the topsoil, creating dust storms. Many of the world's deserts are expanding rapidly, due to weather erosion.

World temperatures today are at their highest recorded level and are continuing to rise. Partly caused by the greenhouse effect, this global warming will seriously affect farming and food production. Low-lying agricultural land will flood if the sea-level rises, while elsewhere good agricultural land will suffer more frequent droughts. As climatic zones shift, so too will the world's major agricultural regions.

An area of rainforest being cleared in Brazil. Over 40 per cent of the world's rainforests have already been destroyed.

ACTIVITY

YOU NEED

- **information from conservation organizations, both international and local, such as Greenpeace and Friends of the Earth**
- **newspaper reports of the spread of deserts and weather disasters**
- **old and new maps of your area**

1 Use the information from conservation organizations to see where the world's forests are being cut down.
2 Why are these forests being destroyed?
3 What is the predicted effect on the climate locally and worldwide?
4 Where in the world are forests being planted?
5 Read reports on the spread of deserts and weather disasters, such as drought, dust storms, river flooding and mud-slides.
6 Find out about local conservation projects. Where are trees used as a windbreak? Is there evidence of soil erosion? Where are woodland areas being destroyed or planted?
7 Look at old maps. How has the ground changed over the years?
8 Write reports of your findings. Display them as an exhibition.

Serious droughts, like this one in New South Wales, Australia, can lead to the death of livestock.

Global warming has already caused the sea-level to rise, leading to more frequent floods in lowland regions.

TEST YOURSELF

1. How do you think that the increase in world population affects the climate?
2. What causes the spread of deserts?
3. What changes have occurred in your area that you think could have some effect on your local climate?

Glossary

Anemometer An instrument for measuring wind speed.

Anticyclone A high-pressure weather system.

Atmosphere The layer of air around the Earth.

Axis An imaginary line about which a given body or system rotates.

Barometer An instrument for measuring atmospheric pressure.

Climate The average weather conditions at any place recorded over a long period of time.

Condense To turn a gas into a liquid. For example to turn water vapour into water by cooling.

Convection current A rising current of air caused by heating. The rising warm air is replaced by cold air. This, in turn, is heated and rises. The warm air cools and falls.

Depression A low-pressure weather system.

Dew point The temperature at which water vapour in the air condenses into droplets of liquid water.

Drizzle Very fine rain, consisting of drops less than 0.5 mm in diameter.

Drought A serious shortage of water.

Erosion The wearing down of land by the action of wind and water, which gradually remove soil or rocks.

Evaporate To change a liquid into a gas. For example, water changes to water vapour when heated.

Front The boundary that separates two large air masses.

Humidity A measure of the amount of water in the air; usually given as a percentage.

Meteorological centre A place where weather forecasts are made from weather information.

Pollution Anything that spoils the environment. Usually, chemicals that foul the air, the land, the rivers and oceans.

Precipitation The name for any condensation falling from clouds.

Reflection Light bouncing off any surface.

Satellite A small object moving around a larger one, such as the Moon around the Earth. Weather satellites are man-made.

Saturate To fill completely. When air is saturated, its humidity is 100 per cent and it will not absorb any more water.

Solstice The time of the year when the Sun reaches its point of furthest distance north or south of the equator.

Static electricity A build-up of electrical charge, usually caused by rubbing (friction).

Supercooled When a liquid is cooled below its normal freezing point, but has not become solid.

Temperate The climatic zone between the polar regions and the tropics. Neither very hot nor very cold.

Thunder The rumble of thunder is actually a 'sonic boom' caused by the extremely rapid expansion of the air around the intensely hot flash of lightning.

Trade winds Tropical winds that blow towards the equator.

Tropics Hot regions of the Earth either side of the equator, between the tropics of Cancer and Capricorn.

Vapour A gas.

Water-table The underground water level; the surface of the water-saturated part of the ground.

Westerlies Temperate winds which blow away from the tropics towards the temperate latitudes.

Books to read

Discovering the Weather Peter Wright
(Longman, 1982)
Looking at Weather Don Radford and Peter
Radford (Batsford, 1986)
The Usborne Book of Weather Facts Anita
Ganeri (Usborne, 1987)
Weather Martyn Bramwell (Franklin Watts,
1987)
Weather John and Mary Gribbin
(Macdonald, 1985)

Weather Mark Pettigrew (Franklin Watts,
1987)
Weather and Climate Keith Lye (Macmillan,
1983)
Weather and Climate John Mason (Wayland,
1988)
Weather and Climate George and Anne
Purvis (Wayland, 1983)
Weather and its Work David Lambert and
Ralph Hardy (Orbis, 1984)

Picture acknowledgements

The author and publishers would like to thank the following for allowing illustrations to be reproduced in this book: Chapel Studios 32 (right); Chris Fairclough Colour Library frontispiece, 16; Hutchison Library 45 (right); A. & M. Meinel 30; Liz Miller 31; NASA 42; TOPHAM 38 (above), 39; Wayland Picture Library 7 (Chris Fairclough), 35, 41, 45 (left/David Bowden); ZEFA cover, 6, 12, 18, 20, 22, 23, 24, 26, 32 (left), 38 (left), 40, 44. Cover artwork by Marilyn Clay. All other artwork by Jenny Hughes.

Index